INTERPERSONAL
SKILLS

INTERPERSONAL SKILLS

Developing Successful Communication

Astrid French

The Industrial Society

First published in 1993 by
The Industrial Society
Robert Hyde House
48 Bryanston Square
London W1H 7LN
Telephone: 071–262 2401

© *The Industrial Society 1993*

ISBN 1 85835 116 2

British Library Cataloguing-in-Publication Data.
A catalogue record for this book is available from the
British Library.

Typeset by: Photoprint Torquay, Devon
Printed by: Bourne Press
Cover design: Pylon

Text illustrations: Sophie Grillet

The Industrial Society is a Registered Charity No. 290003

Communication is the largest single factor determining what kinds of relationships we make with others and what happens to us in the world about us.

Virginia Satir

Contents

Introduction

Interpersonal Skills are what we use when we communicate and deal with other people face-to-face. Everything we say and do to another person will have an effect on them, even though we often don't realise it. Just think for a moment about walking along, seeing someone you know, and they say to you 'Hello' in a friendly way. Now think about them not greeting you at all and avoiding eye contact. Those two simple acts will affect you in totally different ways. Our interpersonal skills can either help or hinder our relationships with other people.

When you communicate with another person you have no choice but to make some impression on each other. When you make the impression you want, your interpersonal effectiveness is high; when you make the impression you don't want, your interpersonal effectiveness is low.

To be successful in terms of interpersonal skills we need to create and maintain good relationships with people, both at work and socially. Maybe you have experienced a time at work when you were very unhappy or even wanted to leave because of a breakdown in relationships with a colleague? Knowing how to handle difficult situations and people will improve your personal effectiveness.

Today at work it is not good enough just to have the technical ability to do the job. Many of us work as part of a team and depend on each other to produce results. It is essential therefore to know how to work well with people in a clear and fair way. Many organisations are now promoting staff because of their 'people skills' rather than on technical ability alone. For you to be successful at work you need the flexibility to deal with a variety of people and situations. Developing your interpersonal effectiveness will allow you to achieve this.

We have all arrived at where we are in life by using the interpersonal skills we have learned based on our experiences and knowledge. Unfortunately we are not taught at school how to act assertively or listen actively even though these are valuable life skills.

No one can make you skilful but yourself. You can read the best book written on 'how to drive a car' but there is no substitute for getting in a car and practising. If you merely read this book, you will miss the point that effective communication is a skill and like all skills must be practised if you want to get better at it. So not only read the exercises in this book but *do* them. By gradually incorporating, in your everyday life, those skills that are appropriate to you and your situation they will feel natural and become part of your repertoire of skills.

When dealing with other people all too often we want *them* to change. It is worth remembering that the only person you can guarantee to change is yourself. We can only hope the other person is willing to change. If you feel a situation will only improve if the other person does something different then you could wait a long time. If we want to improve our relationship with others then we have to find ways of improving our communication and maybe even confronting people with the difficulties we are experiencing with them.

Improving our interpersonal skills takes three steps:

1. Become aware of the way you communicate with others.

2. Develop a broader repertoire of behavioural skills

3. Select the 'right' response at the right time.

These steps require you to be objective and honest about yourself and perhaps to change some of your old habits and replace them with new ones. All communication is learned:, if we realise that then we can set about changing it if we want to. Your aim should be to develop a wide repertoire of ways of dealing with people and situations. If you only rely on the same one or two ways you will only be successful at dealing with a few people. For example, have you ever been abroad on holiday and seen someone trying to speak to a waiter who doesn't speak English. The more they are misunderstood the louder they shout the same thing.

If what you're doing doesn't work – try something different.

Do you see change as a threat or a challenge?

People often say *'I am what I am'*, *'You can't teach an old dog new tricks'*, *'People have to take me or leave me'*. You are what you are but you can change what you **do**. Our personalities are pretty fixed from the age of about seven according to psychologists. Imagine your personality is fixed like a chess board but there's lots of room for manoeuvre and different ways of playing the pieces on the board. You won't win many chess games if you always play the pieces in exactly the same way.

You may find some of the suggestions in this book at odds with what you do at the moment, they may seem strange and uncomfortable. But like all things that are new and different if you practice them after a while they become easier and natural.

> *'Would you tell me please, which way I ought to go from here?'*
> *'That depends a good deal on where you want to get to' said the cat.*
> *'I don't much care where . . .' said Alice.*
> *'Then it doesn't matter which way you go,' said the cat.*
> **Alice in Wonderland, Lewis Carol**

Getting the Most from this Book

You are more likely to get what you want from this book if you know what you want.

1. What do I want?
   Think of what you want rather than what you do not want.

Is it realistic? Is it in harmony with you as a whole person?

Is it at the expense of others?

2. What will I have to give (or give up) to get what I want? Is that realistic?

3. How will I know I have got what I want? What will I see, feel and hear when I have it?

4. Take action.

1

Becoming Aware of How You Communicate

Communication is creating understanding in the minds of others. Effective communicators get their message received in the way they intended it to be received.

Prejudgment can be a barrier to effective communication

When you speak face-to-face with other human beings their senses are taking in what you look like and how you sound. Their brain interprets all this based on their past experiences and view of the world. Meanwhile, you are going through something similar. You don't really know what the other person is feeling, their past or their values. You can only guess unless you check out the facts.

For example: I meet a young man with very short hair and an ear-ring in one ear. I may tell myself that he is a skin-head and as I'm afraid of skin-heads I might feel fear in myself and anger at him. He is looking at me and seeing a middle-aged woman in a smart suit. He may assume I am boring, conservative and not worth bothering with. We are both making assumptions about each other based on our physical appearance at that moment in time.

When running courses for Personnel Officers I have often heard remarks such as '. . . *if the candidate is wearing brown shoes or white socks, he won't get the job'. 'People with Brummie*

accents sound thick'. Research carried out on how candidates are selected for a job shows that interviewers make up their minds within the first few minutes. Interviewers are either negative or positive towards the candidate the first few moments of an interview; from then on every response to a question is interpreted in a way which will confirm that first impression.

Prejudgment can be a useful skill which helps you to categorise the many people you meet. Sometimes it can be accurate but it can also be very wrong. And just like the personnel officer I mentioned, based on very little information you infer a great deal and make instant evaluations. That evaluation then influences how you communicate with that person.

Seven Steps to Improve your Understanding of Others

1. When meeting someone for the first time, resist making your mind up about him/her too soon.

2. Actively listen to the other person and be interested in what s/he has to say.

3. Don't be too influenced by first impressions. Avoid stereotyping people based on their accent and physical appearance, or because they remind you of someone else.

4. Be aware that people behave differently in different situations – just as you do.

5. Avoid looking favourably on people just because they come from the same town, social class, colour, etc. as you do.

6. Try to be as influenced by people's positive points as by their negative points.

7. Judge others after you have heard what they say.

> **Exercise:**
>
> When sitting on the train, watching TV, etc. force yourself to think consciously about the judgments you are making about other people. Are these judgements based on factual knowledge?

Summary

■ Effective communicators get their message received in the way they intended it to be received.

■ If you are not getting the responses you want from others, change your approach.

■ Don't be too influenced by first impressions. Check out the facts before making judgements about others.

Communication is more than words

Research has shown that when we communicate face-to-face, less than 10 per cent of the impact comes from the words we say – Over 90 per cent of the impact is determined by non-verbal communication. Non-verbal communication covers: facial expression, eye contact, gestures, leg movements, body posture, spatial distance, clothes, general appearance and tone of voice.

If you want to be an effective communicator you need to be congruent – that is, your body language and tone of voice should match what you are saying. For example if you want to come across as confident or assertive then you must look and sound it as well as saying the right words, if you want people to believe you.

Test the importance of non-verbal communication on your message out by asking a friend to observe you:

- Talk about how confident you are at a particular job and at the same time fidget with your ring, buttons, etc., look down and bite your lips, shuffle your feet, be hunched rather than upright. Make your tone hesitant and quiet.
- Ask your friend what message she was getting from you and why. She's bound to say 'unconfident' because of the way you looked.

In other words, if you want your message to be received accurately you need to match your tone of voice and body language with the words you say.

Understanding Body Language

'. . . no mortal can keep a secret. If his lips are silent he chatters with his finger tips, betrayal oozes out of him at every pore'.   *Freud*

Understanding body language is essential because over 50 per cent of our message's impact comes from body language. Another good reason to take notice of it is that it often gives you more information than the words people are saying. Have you ever given someone instructions about something and watched their eyes glaze over and a puzzled look come over their face? If you ask *'do you understand?'* and they say *'yes'* you will probably not believe them and carry on trying to explain.

We are all mini-experts in reading body language, as we have been learning it since we were very young. You didn't learn from reading in a book that when someone is towering over you, anf their eyes are piercing into yours, their teeth are clenched and so are their fists, then they are being aggressive.

However, to be effective communicators we need to improve our awareness of other people's and our own body language. Becoming more aware of your own visual behaviour will help you choose behaviours which will help rather than hinder your dealings with others.

Helen was a union rep, and she claimed every time she went to see her manager about anything there was always an argument. She could not understand why and was unhappy about the situation. She said she was a friendly person and couldn't understand why there was always an argument.

Helen was asked to role-play how she went into her manager's office. She proceeded to roll-up her sleeves, put her hands on her hips and march into his office with a jutting chin and fixed gaze.

Helen was totally unaware of her body language and the message it was giving to her manager.

By changing her visual behaviour she changed her manager's behaviour towards her.

It is possible to misunderstand people's body language by trying to interpret a single gesture in isolation from other gestures. For example, people will tell me someone is being defensive just because they have their arms folded across their body. It may well be the person is cold or just relaxed, depending on the other gestures that occur at the same time and the context in which they occur. So if someone is sitting in a cold waiting-room and they have their legs and arms tightly crossed, their head and eyes looking down, the probability is that they are cold. If they were sitting opposite you in a negotiation situation, it could well mean they were being defensive or negative.

The same goes for you, if you do just one thing in isolation it probably won't have the right effect. Watch what people are doing with their:

- facial expressions and head movements
- gestures with hands and arms
- rest of body and legs.

Culture can be a source of mis-communication

A problem in understanding non-verbal communication is that the meaning of many movements and gestures are

culturally determined. Just as verbal language differs from one culture to another, so too can non-verbal language. These differences can lead to quite serious misunderstandings. For example research carried (out by Gumpertz *et al*, 1979) found that the way Asian people speak English in Britain can lead to incorrect judgements of aggressiveness being made about them. People from the Mediterranean generally stand closer, touch more and engage in more eye contact than English people. In some cultures you look down as a mark of respect when a more senior person is questioning you. In England we may perceive that as 'shifty' and say *'look at me when I'm speaking to you'*.

To improve your understanding of body language and therefore what people are thinking, spend time observing people's gestures and read a book on the subject. I recommend Allan Pease's *Body Language – How to read others' thoughts by their gestures*.

UNCONFIDENT AND UNASSERTIVE	AGGRESSIVE	CONFIDENT AND ASSERTIVE
FACIAL EXPRESSION		
Unreal smile when expressing anger, or being criticised; eyebrows raised in anticipation (e.g. of rebuke); quick-changing features.	Smile may become 'wry'; scowls when angry; eyebrows raised in amazement/disbelief; jaws set firm; chin thrust forward.	Smiles when pleased; frowns when angry; otherwise 'open' features steady not wobbling; jaw relaxed but not 'loose'.
EYE CONTACT		
Evasive, looking down.	Tries to stare down and dominate.	Firm but not a 'stare-down'.
BODY MOVEMENT		
Hand wringing; hunching shoulders; stepping back; covering mouth with hand; nervous movements which detract (shrugs and shuffles).	Finger pointing; fist thumping; sits upright or leans forward; stands upright; strides impatiently; arms crossed (unapproachable); stands with head straight.	Open hand movements (inviting to speak); measured pace hand movements; sits upright or relaxed (not slouching or cowering).
VOICE		
Sometimes wobbly; tone may be sing-song or whining; over-soft or over-warm; often dull and monotone.	Very firm; tone is sarcastic; sometimes cold, hard and sharp; strident, often shouting.	Steady and firm; tone is middle range; range, rich and warm; sincere and clear; not too loud or quiet.
SPEECH PATTERN		
Hesitant and filled with pauses; sometimes jerks from fast to slow; frequent throat clearing.	Fluent, few awkward hesitances; often abrupt, clipped; emphasises blaming words.	Fluent, few awkward hesitances; emphasises key words; steady, even pace.

Proxemics

Proxemics is the study of what you communicate by the way you use space. Just as animals stake out and guard their territory, so do humans. Apart from the personal territory which exists around our homes and possessions, we also have a defined space around our bodies. The anthropologist Edward T. Hall was one of the pioneers in the study of man's spatial needs and he described four distinct zones that people unconsciously use as they interact with others:

(1) **intimate zone**   15–46cm
(2) **personal zone**   46cm–1.2m
(3) **social zone**   1.2–3.6m and
(4) **public zone**   over 3.6m.

It's as if we have four concentric bubbles around us. The size of the bubbles depend on the density of the population in the place where you grew up and from culture to culture.

Research has shown that people from South America, the Mediterranean and Japan maintain closer proximity than people from Northern Europe and North America. City dwellers usually have smaller territorial bubbles than people from the countryside who are used to living much further apart from their neighbours. Generally speaking, the greater the distance between two people interacting, the less intimate their relationship.

Intimate zone – we allow people into our intimate zone who are close friends, lovers or children but feel embarrassed or threatened if we are forced to share this zone with people we are not intimate with.

We cope with this by avoiding eye contact and touch. Next

time you are in a crowded lift or train, observe how people assiduously avoid eye contact and pull back and tense up if they are accidentally touched.

Personal zone – this is a comfortable zone for talking to people at parties and social gatherings.

Social zone – this is the distance we stand with strangers, clients or service people and with work colleagues we do not know well.

Public zone – when the boss is talking to the staff, or when we have to address a large group of people.

If you want people to feel comfortable in your company don't stand too close unless you have an intimate relationship with them.

Katherine was interviewing people for a job. An Italian man came into the interview room and moved his chair much closer to Katherine than she felt happy with; she also felt intimidated by his eye contact. Katherine was unwilling to employ the man because she felt he was a 'Romeo'. She subsequently found out that she had wrongly judged the man by not understanding the cultural differences in proxemics and body language.

Exercise:

Stand in the middle of a room and have a friend walk towards you. Tell them to stop when you feel they are at a comfortable distance from you. Does this distance change with different people?

Observe other people's reaction to you when you stand very close to them. (Be careful when you do this exercise.)

It's Not What You Say But the Way That You Say It

'In the right key one can say anything. In the wrong key, nothing: the only delicate part is the establishment of the key'.   **Shaw**

Research has shown that over a third of the impact of our communication comes from our tone of voice. However, most of us are not aware of how we sound when we talk or the impact it has on our message.

Think of all the different shades of meaning you can get with the simple word 'yes': bored and fed up, excited, questioning. People's tone of voice can have a big impact on us. You can be feeling very relaxed and happy as you walk into work but your boss comes up to you and says *'Will you step into my office please?'*. The tone is controlled anger. Do you still feel relaxed and happy? When my daughter Hannah is playing in the garden and I call her in, she knows by the way I call her name whether I am pleased or angry with her.

Sometimes it's our tone of voice which affects our relationships with others. Think about some of the people you seem to rub up the wrong way or who rub you up the wrong way – could tone of voice be the culprit?

Think about the tone you are using when dealing with others. If you don't care about the other person or are feeling bored, your tone of voice will convey that message. Changing your tone could change their response.

Exercise:

Ask a friend or partner how your voice sounds to them.
Listen to your voice on a tape-recorder. Can you convey happiness, enthusiasm, boredom, anger? Or is there very little difference in the tone. As you listen to yourself on tape ask yourself:

- Does your voice reflect what you want to say?
- Do your tone and words match?
- Is there something about your voice you would like to change?

Vary your voice and keep in mind how you would like it to sound. If people have difficulty understanding you when you speak, practise speaking louder or softer, slower or faster. Read out passages from a book and practise drawing out the vowel sounds and exaggerating the consonants. This may sound strange to do but it is possible to train your voice to sound different. After all your voice is a wind instrument and the sounds you get out of it depend on how you use it.

Sending Your Message Effectively

1. **Decide what you are going to say.**

   'Own' your message by using 'I', 'my' words. Owning your message means taking responsibility for the ideas and feelings that you express. People disown their message when they say things like *'most people think that'*, or *'one has to control one's emotions'*.

2. **Get the other person's attention**

   Are they looking at you? Beware of distractions – phones ringing, others speaking, lots of noise going on.

3. **Use language they will understand**

   Have you used words or jargon they are unfamiliar with? Is it appropriate to their level of understanding? You need to explain things differently to your boss or a new member of staff.

4. **Make your verbal and non-verbal messages congruent**
   Every face-to-face communication involves both verbal and non-verbal messages. Problems arise when you say one thing, but look like you mean something else. For example saying *'Can I help you?'* with a bored look and monotone voice. The receiver is confused by two different messages being sent.

5. **Check for understanding**
   If you only *assume* someone has understood you, then you risk being misunderstood. Feedback from the other person will tell you if you have to change what you are saying or whether it is OK. In any case check by asking questions and observing their body language to make sure they have understood you.

6. **If you're not getting the response you want** – change your approach.

Summary

- Develop an awareness of your own and others' body language.
- The tone you use has a greater impact than the words you say.
- Ensure the distance between yourself and the person you are speaking to is consistent with your relationship.
- Your listener will receive a confused message unless your tone of voice and body language matches your words.

Behaviour Breeds Behaviour

Our body language, our tone of voice and everything people can see and hear about us is our behaviour. The way we behave towards other people is very important because judgements about us are based on what they can see and hear. We make judgements about other people in exactly the same way. We cannot see inside another human being, their feelings, hopes, fears, beliefs, motives and they cannot see inside us All we have to go on is what we can see and hear – their behaviour.

Think of a time recently, either at work or socially, when someone approached you in an aggressive way. How did you behave? Did you automatically become aggressive or defensive? If you did, then you just allowed *someone else's* behaviour to control *your* behaviour. It is very easy to get hooked into other people's behaviour and allow them to control the situation.

Just as someone else's behaviour can have an affect on your behaviour, so your behaviour can affect and shape other people's behaviour. Your behaviour is therefore a tool which can help or hinder your dealings with other people.

How do we deal with other people's difficult behaviour?

When you are having to deal with difficult behaviour it is all too easy to react to that person by saying and doing the first thing that comes into your head. We often then regret what we said or did, and the feelings of saying or doing the wrong thing lives on for much longer than the event itself.

The key to dealing successfully with difficult people and not allowing their behaviour to control you, is to avoid the emotional traps their behaviour often puts you in. You will know you have been trapped or 'hooked' by:

- saying things in anger and later regretting it
- seething silently inside and saying nothing
- reacting in ways that are uncharacteristic and disliking yourself for it.

A good way to stop yourself being hooked is to recognise what is happening and then follow the 'green cross code':

■ **Stop** – suppress your emotions for a moment and take a deep breath
say to yourself – *'my behaviour can affect the outcome'*
'I can choose how to behave'
'I have the power to control what I say and how I feel'

■ **Look** – at the other person's behaviour
their body language – (their words may be saying one thing and their body something else)

■ **Listen** – to exactly what they are saying
the meaning and feelings behind the words.

Then respond, don't react. You now have a choice: you can either be in charge of how you behave towards them or you can get hooked into their behaviour.

A way of responding that I have found useful in this kind of situation is to separate the *person* from the *issue*. Tackle *issues* not *people*. In my experience situations where people attack each other's personalities are unproductive and end in unnecessary conflict. If it happens at work you could well look foolish and out of control to your colleagues. Try concentrating on the necessity to build a working relationship with this person and attempt to ignore aspects of their personality you don't like. But be careful, you have to look and sound as though you mean it, otherwise people won't believe you. It's easy to say the right words but be totally unconvincing because your visual behaviour is saying something different.

John had a particular colleague who often spoke to him regarding work in a sarcastic and critical way. John would become defensive and 'give as good as he got'. John wanted to change the situation as it was causing him stress and he did not like the fact his manager viewed the situation as a personality clash.

John decided not to get sucked into his colleague's behaviour when he approached him, by taking a deep breath and responding not reacting. He now deals firmly with the work issue and does not allow himself to become defensive. John now feels much more in control of the situation, and his collague's behaviour is being forced to change because John's behaviour is changing.

Remember you are in charge of your own feelings and behaviour and therefore you always have a choice about how to behave. What may influence your choice is whether you will ever see that person again, or whether tomorrow or sometime in the future you may need help or cooperation from them.

Think about your own relationships with people. Are there any that really frustrate you? Is there someone at work who you need to establish a working relationship with but who resists being cooperative whenever you approach them.?

The trick is to expand your range of behaviour so you can direct the situation to what **you** want and not let **their** behaviour control you. What normally happens when we encounter resistance is that we push harder with more of the same approach. If what you're doing isn't working then you need the flexibility to change and to try a different approach. The message here is: *If you want to change someone else's behaviour, try changing your own.*

Of course there is no magic guarantee that by changing your behaviour you will automatically be able to change everyone else's. There will always be people who resist you whatever you do. But by becoming more flexible in your approaches to others you can greatly increase your inter-personal effectiveness.

Exercise:

Is there someone you find it difficult to deal with and would like to change the situation?

Difficult Person/Difficult Situation Questionnaire

1. How frequently do these types of situations occur with this person?

    sometimes ☐   always ☐

2. Could you be biased about the situation?

    ■ are you being objective – would you know if you weren't?
    ■ do other people find this person difficult and have the same problems with them that you do?

3. What does the difficult person feel about you?

    ■ would they consider you to be a difficult person?
    ■ do you have any habits, attitudes or behaviours that might be considered difficult?

4. What changes are you looking for?

5. What can you do to help change the situation?

Plan of Action

1. Why does this person make me feel the way I do?

2. What *specifically* does this person do to make me feel this way?

3. What is my normal response to them?
    – tone of voice, choice of words, body language.
    – do I listen?

4. What will I do now, that I haven't tried before with this person? (As my previous behaviours haven't worked.)

Practise what you are going to do and then do it.

Summary

- People make judgements about us based on what they can see and hear.
- Your behaviour can affect and shape other people's behaviour.
- Respond, don't react.
- Tackle issues not people.
- If what you're doing isn't working, try a different approach.

Transactional Analysis

A framework for understanding our own and other people's behaviour is Transactional Analysis. Dr. Eric Berne, a psychiatric therapist, developed a theory in the 1950s about personality and personality development. The theory states that all the feelings and experiences people are exposed to during infancy and childhood are unconsciously recorded in the brain. These recorded messages greatly influence our behaviour for the rest of our lives.

Berne suggested that every human being has three ego states: Parent, Adult and Child. You can be operating out of any one of these ego states at any time. Think about yourself for a moment. If you have children have you ever listened to yourself telling them off and realised you are speaking in the same way your mother or father told you off? And you promised yourself you would be different from your parents! Have you experienced hearing a piece of music or smelling a smell which took you back to when you were a child? Or using a piece of equipment that doesn't work properly and throwing it on the floor in a tantrum? It is as if within each person there is the little three-year-old person you once were and your own parents.

The Parent

The Parent in everyone is a huge collection of rules and instructions that your parents or the big people in your life, provided you with. Because of our smallness and dependency at that time, the assumption was that they were right. If you sometimes talk to yourself saying things like *'That was a stupid thing to do'* or *'You did really well there'*, your Parent is telling your Child off or praising your Child.

You express a **Parent** ego state when you:

give advise, criticise, discipline, moralise, nurture and protect make rules and regulations, teach, judge.

The Child

The Child consists of recordings of information stored in our brains from early life. All your urges to know, to feel, to touch and to experience a new world. Our feelings of frustration, confusion and anger when we were told off by the 'big' people. Your Child is divided into two parts: the Adapted Child is expressed when you go into an automatic behaviour pattern to enable you to get some response from

BY ALL MEANS STOOP,
BUT PLEASE — NO LINGUISTIC
IMBECILITY

the 'big people' in your life. The Free Child is expressed through spontaneity without concern for the reactions of the 'big people'.

The **Child** ego state is observable when you show:

■ fear, anger, rebelliousness, curiosity, creativity, trust love, excitement, self-indulgence, aggression, servility.

The Adult

This is the part of you that figures things out by collecting and looking at the facts of a situation. The Adult seeks information, respects other people, is constructive and non-dogmatic.

You use your **Adult** when you:

■ store information, plan, check alternatives, make decisions, reason, recall information, evaluate, estimate probabilities, set limits.

You can become acquainted with your own Parent Adult and Child ego states by listening to these three different voices inside yourself.

These three ego states are within us all the time. When we act, speak or make gestures that are influenced by our parents' behaviour, we are acting from our 'Parent'. Our 'Child' within us influences emotions and spontaneous behaviour. The 'Adult' state collects and organises information, predicts the consequences of various actions and makes decisions. Using the Adult ego state can increase a person's potential for success.

Most people are unaware of these ego states, yet all human communication is made to and from Parent, Adult or Child. By becoming aware and learning to recognise the Parent, Adult and Child behaviours in ourselves and others, we can greatly improve the quality of communications.

The skill of Transactional Analysis is learning to identify whether you are talking from your Parent, Adult or Child.

Identify the following statements as those from either Parent, Adult, or Child:

1. *This photocopier isn't working, I'd like to jump on it.*

2. *Stop moping around, smarten yourself up.*

3. *You ought to know better.*

INDICATIONS OF EGO STATES:

	Critical Parent	Nurturing Parent	Adult	Free Child	Adapted Child
WORDS	bad should ought always ridiculous	good nice I love you splendid tender	correct how what practical quantity	wow fun want ouch hi	can't wish try please thank you
VOICE	critical condescending disgusted	loving comforting concerned	even	free loud energetic	whinny defiant placating
GESTURES/ EXPRESSIONS	points finger frowns angry	open arms accepting smiling	thoughtful alert open	uninhibited loose spontaneous	pouting sad innocent
STYLE	judgement moralistic authoritarian	understanding caring giving	erect evaluation of facts	curious fun-loving changeable	demanding compliant ashamed

4. *Why do I always have to get the coffee?.*

5. *When you're going to be late home John, I'd appreciate a call.*

6. *In my day, workers knew how to work.*

7. *Check with Mrs. Smith, she may know where the file has been put.*

Answers: 1) C, 2) P, 3) P, 4) C, 5) A, 6) P, 7) A

As you become more skilled in spotting Parent, Adult and Child characteristics in others, you will also become more aware of them in yourself. You can also get some clues about how you come across to others by identifying how they react to you.

For example: a colleague at work reacts to something you have just said with *'Well I was only trying to be helpful. If you don't like what I'm doing, do it yourself'*. You might learn something about yourself by playing back what it was you said (or the way you said it) which provoked the reaction. Your colleague may have felt put down or criticised by what you said. Subconsciously your colleague heard your Parent talking, and responded with his Child ego.

Thomas Harris, a follower of Eric Berne, in his book *I'm OK You're OK* suggests ways for analysing your communication and building a strong Adult:

1. **Learn to recognise your Child**, its vulnerabilities, its fears and its principal methods of expressing these feelings. Exercise your Child by showing enthusiasm and responding with energy and interest when people are talking to you.

2. **Learn to recognise your Parent**, its rules, fixed ideas and primary ways of expressing these commands and positions.

3. **Be sensitive to the Child in others** – respond to it by giving praise, smiling, saying the person's name, and giving attention.

4. **Count to ten, if necessary**, in order to give the Adult time to sort out Parent and Child from reality.

5. **If in doubt, leave it out** – If something is difficult and what you are about to say does not compute clearly in your Adult, don't say it. You can't be attacked for what you didn't say.

To find out more about how to use Transactional Analysis to understand and improve your communication with others read *I'm OK You're OK* by Thomas A. Harris.

2

Developing A Broader Repertoire

Developing an Assertive Style

What do we mean by assertiveness?

Assertive behaviour is about expressing your feelings, thoughts and wishes, and standing up for your own basic rights without violating the basic rights of others. It's about saying what you mean and having self-respect and respect for others. Assertiveness is a skill you can acquire – not a personality trait.

Nobody is consistently assertive. You may find it easy to be assertive with strangers but very difficult with your family or work colleagues. If you would like to act more assertively, particularly in difficult or stressful situations, then you need to acquire a positive self-image and to believe that you can act effectively.

Why Behave Assertively?

The ability to express feelings constructively and to be open to others about what you want, maximises the chances of you getting more of the life you want. If you are usually passive you are likely to get trampled on by other people and this will lower your self-respect and self-esteem; aggression usually leads to people avoiding you. Paradoxically aggressive people also have low self-esteem because they are often uncertain of their own position and simply use aggression as the best method of defence.

By acting assertively we get more of what we want out of situations, which in turn builds up our self-esteem and gives us the confidence to go on acting assertively. So it is important to be assertive not only to get more of what you want but also to feel better about yourself and your behaviour.

Answer honestly the questionnaire that follows on pages 38 and 39. It will give you some insight in how assertive you already are.

What are Non-assertive and Assertive Behaviours?

Aggressive behaviour

(It is important to be able to distinguish genuine anger from aggression. Aggressive behaviour is often used as a form of manipulation, to punish and place blame rather than to deal with the situation and resolve it):

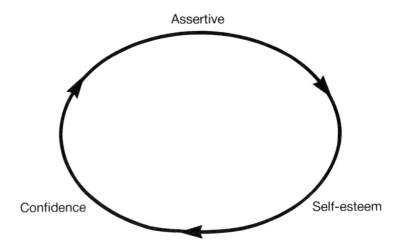

- Violates rights, takes advantage of others.

- May achieve goals at expense of others.

- Defensive, belligerent, humiliates others.

- Explosive; unpredictable hostile and angry.

- Intrudes on the choices of others.

Passive behaviour

(Passivity is often related to a sense of powerlessness and feeling you can have no influence over what happens):

- Has rights violated; is taken advantage of.

- Does not achieve goals.

- Feels frustrated, unhappy, hurt and anxious.

- Inhibited and withdrawn.

- Allows others to choose for him or her.

HOW ASSERTIVE ARE YOU?

	1 Often	2 Some-times	3 Rarely	4 Never
1 In a difficult meeting with tempers running high I am able to speak up with confidence.				
2 If I am unsure of something I can easily ask for help.				
3 If someone is being unfair and aggressive I can handle the situation confidently.				
4 When someone is being sarcastic at my expense or at the expense of others, I can speak up without getting angry.				
5 If I am being put down or patronised I can raise the issue directly without being aggressive.				
6 If I believe I am being taken for granted I am able to draw attention to it without sulking or getting upset.				
7 If someone asks my permission to do something I would prefer them not to, e.g. smoke, I can say no without feeling guilty.				
8 If someone asks my opinion about something, I feel quite comfortable to give it, even if I think my opinion will not be a popular one.				
9 I can deal easily and effectively with senior people.				
10 When given faulty or substandard goods in a shop or restaurant I can state my case well without attacking the other person.				

HOW ASSERTIVE ARE YOU?

	1 Often	2 Some- times	3 Rarely	4 Never
11 When an important opportunity is in the offing I can speak up on my own account.				
12 When I can see things going wrong I can draw attention to it early without waiting until it is a potential disaster.				
13 When I have bad news to give I can do it calmly and without excessive worry.				
14 If I want something I can ask for it in a direct, straight-forward way.				
15 When someone isn't listening to what I'm saying, I can get my point across without getting strident or feeling sorry for myself.				
16 When someone misunderstands me, I can point it out without feeling guilty or making the other person look small.				
17 When I disagree with the majority view I can state my case without apologising or getting high-handed.				
18 I take criticism well.				
19 I give compliments without being embarrassed or sounding like flattery.				
20 When I get angry, I can express my point of view without becoming judgemental or feeling I've let myself down.				

How to score

20–25   You are confident and assertive in your approach to situations

26–35   Although you can be assertive you would benefit from assertiveness training

36–50   You are unable to be consistent in your assertive behaviours and should work to improve this

51–80   You need to do some considerable work to develop assertive behaviour

Assertive behaviour

■ Allow others to complete what they are saying before speaking.

■ Stand up for the position that matches our feelings or the evidence.

■ Make our own decisions on what we think is right.

■ Can spontaneously enter into conversation using a moderate tone and volume of voice.

■ Try to understand the feelings of others before describing our own.

■ Try to avoid harm or inconvenience to ourselves and

others by talking through problems before they occur or finding rational means for coping with them when they do.

■ Face problems and decisions squarely.

■ Consider ourselves strong and capable but generally equal to most other people.

■ Face responsibility with respect to our situation, needs and rights.

Some people may feel they would like to act more assertively, but that by behaving differently others would see them in a different light. As we are all very attached to our personal identities we often fear that acting assertively might somehow change who we really are. Before going on, ask yourself if it is really worth it to you to change. Think about the following questions:

1. **How does acting passively benefit you?**
   If you behaved assertively instead, what would you have to give up?

2. **How does acting aggressively benefit you?**
   If you behaved assertively instead, what would you have to give up?

3. **Make a list of what you would gain by being assertive.**

_____

_____

_____

_____

_____

_____

_____

_____

Why Rights are Important to Assertiveness

Rights are important because they are one of the bases for deciding whether other people are behaving aggressively, passively or assertively towards you. If you do not know what your rights are then you will find it hard to judge whether other people are violating your rights.

Bill of Rights

Below is a Bill of Rights which I support. You may want to create your own. But remember the rights you want for yourself you must also extend to others.

Which of the statements below do you agree with?
Circle T for True, F for False and ? for Don't Know.

Everyone has the right:

1. To hold and express different views
   from other people   T   F   ?

2. To be listened to and taken
    seriously   T   F   ?

3. To say 'no'   T   F   ?

4. To disagree   T   F   ?

5. To be treated with respect   T   F   ?

6. To admit ignorance   T   F   ?

7. To set their own priorities   T   F   ?

8. To express anger   T   F   ?

9. To privacy   T   F   ?

10. To be wrong   T   F   ?

Rights & Responsibilities

Unfortunately rights don't exist on their own, we have responsibilities that go with them. For example if you want the right to be listened to and taken seriously, then you have to do the same for others.

At work you may say *'I have the right to make mistakes from time to time'*. The responsibilities that go with this right are:

– To acknowledge a mistake and not blame others
– To put it right
– To learn from it and not continually repeat it
– To acknowledge others make mistakes

Be aware of becoming over-assertive in certain situations, particularly at work. You will come across as arrogant if you seem over-concerned with your rights and less concerned about others. Be aware of the culture of your organisation or team: implementing assertive skills may give you difficulties in the short term. This should not discourage you from being assertive but enable you to recognise that colleagues may become antagonistic towards you. Being successfully assertive is knowing how to judge situations and acting appropriately.

Before facing a situation ask yourself:

'What are my rights?'
'What are the rights of the other person?'
'Does that person accept my rights?'
'Do I accept that person's rights?'

Exercise:

Think of a recent situation where you did not act assertively:

■ What was the incident?

■ What did you say and do?

■ How do you now feel about it?

Thinking Positively

Have you ever wanted to do something but a little voice inside your head said *'No, don't do it'*, *'You'll fail'*, *'You're not good enough'*, *'Your ideas are useless, stupid'*.

That's negative inner dialogue! Turn the voice down or ignore it. It is important to have positive expectations otherwise it could be a self-fulfilling prophecy. Imagine two runners about to run a 100 metres race: runner A's inner voice is saying *'You'll never do it, you'll lose, you'll trip over'*. Runner B's voice is saying *'You're going to do it, you are going to win, you will be successful'*. Which one will you bet on to win?

We often succeed or fail because subconsciously we know we will. Our expectations can have a powerful impact on the eventual outcome. This is not about seeing everything through rose-tinted glasses or thinking that by *saying* you will succeed you actually *will*. Have confidence in your own abilities and judgements and replace negative inner dialogue with some positive inner dialogue. If you do not respect yourself and your views, how can other people? Take a leaf out of Muhammad Ali's book (probably the most famous boxer ever). He told everyone he was 'the greatest' and we believed him!

Think back over the past couple of weeks and choose two situations – one in which you were confident and successful and one in which you were not:

Successful situation:

– What was my behaviour?

– What was my inner dialogue?

– How did I feel?

Unsuccessful situation

– What was my behaviour?

– What was my inner dialogue?

– How did I feel?

In the future, what would I need to do to make more situations successful?

First Rule of Assertiveness
– Know others have rights

– decide what you want to say and say it clearly and concisely

– be prepared to change your mind

– look for a win-win situation where appropriate

Assertive Responses

Basic assertion is simply standing up for your rights.

'I'd like to finish what I'm saying'

'I'd like to finish this phone call, then I will speak to you'.
(*aggressive*: **'can't you see I'm on the phone'?**)

'I would like this replaced, it's broken'.

'Why did that happen'
(*aggressive/blaming*: **'why did you do that'?**)

'I'm unhappy about this decision'.
(*aggressive*: **'You've made a stupid decision'**).

Assertive statements need to be said in the right tone. Your voice should be even, firm but friendly, otherwise you may be perceived as being aggressive.

You can soften these statements and still remain assertive:

e.g.   *'I know you're very busy at the moment, but I bought this here yesterday and it's now broken. Will you please replace it?'*

'I appreciate you have strong views on this issue and I will listen to them. However I would like to finish what I am saying.'

A good formula for an assertive statement is to use the following three steps:

1.   *Show the other person you understand things from their view* (don't confuse this with saying you agree with them).
2.   *Say what you feel or think.*
3.   *Say what you want to happen.*

e.g.   *'Jim, I appreciate you have strong views on this issue and I will listen to them. However when you keep interrupting me it makes me feel irritated and annoyed. You can give your views after I have finished.'*

or

'I understand why you feel Mary is the best candidate for the job. On the other hand, I feel Jane is better qualified. Let's bring them both back for a second interview.'

Step one forces you to listen to the other person and demonstrate understanding and empathy. You can appreciate and understand their view without agreeing with them.

Step two enables you to state your thoughts and feelings in an non-apologetic way. Own your feelings, thoughts, perceptions by using 'I' statements.

Step three is a way of indicating clearly what action or outcome you want.

Jane was recently promoted over Mary, an older woman who has worked in the department for longer than Jane. Mary became very resentful, unfriendly and uncooperative. Jane was feeling undermined and very tense about the whole situation. She did not know the best way to handle it. After attending an IPS course, Jane decided on her plan of action. She called Mary into her office and in a calm, even voice explained how she felt about their working relationship and how she would like it to improve. Jane listened carefully to Mary and encouraged her to say how she felt. Jane's relationship with Mary is now much better. Jane feels she tackled the issue while at the same time being sensitive to Mary's feelings. In future when Jane deals with her staff she will be aware of:

Body language: In the past Jane's body language looked as if she was being apologetic for being the supervisor. She will now stand straight, relaxed and give people good eye contact.

Vocal/Verbal: In an even natural voice she will ask people to do things without sounding unsure of herself, e.g. '*I need this typed for tomorrow*' or '*Can you check the figures?*' said as a statement and not as if she is also asking the question – 'Is that all right with you?'

Exercise:

Look at the example situations below and see if you can identify the responses as either **Aggressive (Ag)**, **Passive (P)** or **Assertive (A)**:

	Situation	Response	Your answer
1.	A colleague interrupts you when you are making a call to a customer. You say:	*'I'd like to finish this phone call then I'll be with you'*	
2.	A colleague in another department has volunteered your services without consulting you. You say:	*'What a nerve! Why didn't you ask me first? There's no way I can help out. I'm up to my eyes as it is. You'll have to manage on your own.'*	
3.	Your boss has sent a memo saying that no more business visits are to be made without her prior agreement. You are unhappy with this and say:	*'Jane, I'm unhappy with the new arrangement. The way I see it, it takes away my professional judgement. I'd like to discuss it with you.'*	

4.	A colleague agreed to come to a special meeting but then failed to turn up. You ring him and say:	*'Well, I suppose it didn't matter that you weren't there. We managed all right without you in the end.'*
5.	A salesperson has been pushing hard for you to buy a piece of equipment. You are not too sure; besides you had thought of looking at several makes before making a decision. You say:	*'Well I guess it's more or less what I'm looking for. I was going to look at other makes but perhaps this will be OK'.*
6.	Your boss is about the leave the office for an important meeting. You need to ask him if you may work at home tomorrow. You say:	*'I know you're in a rush John, but I'd like to make a quick request of you.'*
7.	Your secretary is arranging your diary for the day. She asks you 'What time will you be back in the office'? You say:	*'When you see me walk through that door.'*

8.	One of your colleagues (you don't know which one) forgot to pass on an important message to you. You take this up with your boss. You say:	*'This department is completely hopeless. They can't even write down a simple message. What are you going to do about it?'*
9.	The date is being set for the next team meeting. You are keen to attend but the proposed date clashes with another appointment. You say:	*'Well all right, it seems to be convenient for everyone else.'*

(1–A, 2–Ag, 3–A, 4–Ag, 5–P, 6–A, 7–Ag, 8–Ag, 9–P)

Other Assertive Techniques

Broken Record

This is a useful technique to us when you feel someone isn't really listening to you, for example, in conflict situations, when refusing unreasonable requests, when saying no, when correcting someone, when being taken advantage of.

What you do:

You speak as if you were a broken record. You need to be persistent by sticking to the main point of what you are saying and repeating it calmly and without blaming. It is important to keep repeating the message using some of the same words over and over again in different sentences. This reinforces your message and stops you getting side-tracked by red herrings. Broken records eventually get heard; it's uncomfortable to listen for too long.

e.g. You: *'I would like my money back. This jumper has a hole in it.'*
Shop Assistant: *'Sorry, I didn't serve you'.*
You: *'I know you didn't serve me. However, I'd like my money back on this jumper.'*
Shop Assistant: *'We have lots of other jumpers'*
You: *'I don't think you heard me. I'd like my money back'.*

Workable Compromise
There are three solutions to any problem:
- My solution
- Your solution
- OUR solution

In most work or home situations it is rare that you have all the answers or the monopoly on the truth. If I am only prepared to stick to *my* solution and you to *yours*, we will end up either in stalemate or with one or other of us being forced to back down. Looking for a workable 'win-win' compromise will break any deadlock and both parties will win a bit and give up a bit. This is much better than having to back down.

e.g. Customer: *'We want the 100 tables delivered on Monday'.*
You: *'Sorry, we can't. We can deliver on Wednesday'.*
Customer: *'I must have them on Monday'.*
You: *'We can't get them to you till Wednesday'.*

Either this conversation will go round and round with both of you getting more and more exasperated until one of you finally gives in, or you can go for a workable compromise:–

e.g. You: (workable compromise) *'What if we delivered half of the tables on Monday and the balance on Wednesday?'*
Customer: *'That may be a possibility, let's discuss it'.*

Learning to be assertive doesn't mean that you must always behave assertively. If someone is about to mug you, it is entirely appropriate to become aggressive. Learning to be assertive means that you have the choice about when and where to assert yourself.

Summary

- express your feelings, attitudes, wishes, opinions or rights directly and honestly
- respect the feelings, attitudes, wishes, opinions and rights of the other person
- do not violate the rights of others
- look for 'win-win' solutions where possible
- you do not have to behave assertively in every situation
- whatever choice you make, keep in mind the consequences of your action.

'One who is too insistent on his own views, finds few to agree with him'.

Lao-Tsu, Tao Teh King

Yes, But . . .

Certain phrases and words we use can cause resistance in other people. When we say to another person *'Yes, but . . .'*, what we really mean is *'No, I disagree'*. How do you feel when people say *'I agree, but . . .'*? How many times have you heard conversations like this:

'I think it would be a good idea if we did . . .'
'Yes, but . . .'
'Yes, but I still think . . .'
'Yes, but . . .'

This can go on for ever, with each person digging their heels in and not really listening to the other person or looking for a 'win-win' solution. If you listen for something you can agree with in the other person's ideas, and then simply substitute 'and' for 'but', you have kept the channels of communication open instead of creating resistance in the other person. Here is an example of two approaches, the 'Yes, but' and the 'Yes, and':

e.g.   You: *'We need to come up with a new colour for the product'.*
Colleague: *'What about yellow, that's a bright, eye-catching colour'.*
You: *'Yes, but yellow gets dirty easily and customers don't like it'.*

Colleague: *(shuts up and sulks. He feels put down because his idea was put down).*

Try instead the following approach:

You: *'Yes, Fred, we do need something bright and eye-catching. Can you come up with another colour which gets over the cleaning problems customers associate with yellow?'.*

You don't have to agree with the content of the other person's communication, but if you say *'I disagree'* or *'You're wrong'*, the chances of them listening to you further are pretty remote. You can always appreciate or respect another's feelings. Saying instead, *'I appreciate you feel strongly about this, and I believe you may feel differently if you hear my point of view'*, may keep them listening and more open.

It is easier to persuade people from agreement to agreement than from disagreement to agreement. Avoid resistance by looking for something you can agree with and build on in what the other person says.

> **Exercise:**
>
> Get together with a friend and choose a topic which you can each take opposite sides. Both argue your case trying to avoid using the word 'but' and without putting the other person's views down. Look for something in their argument you can build on. This does not mean you have to give up your views. It may demonstrate that no-one has the monopoly on truth.

Active Listening

We can improve our understanding of other people's behaviour and increase our own ability to make and keep friendships by learning the skills of active listening.

Good listening requires a set of skills:

- the ability to concentrate on what the other person is saying
- a willingness to empathise with the other person (seeing things from their viewpoint)
- Picking up on the feelings behind the words

Good listeners get listened to.

We are all guilty of putting up barriers to active listening.

Recognise any of those?

1. Not listening to everything the other person is saying because we are too busy working out what we are going to say next.

2. Only hearing what we want to hear. We avoid listening to negative, unpleasant or critical statements.

3. Pre-judging what they are saying before they have finished speaking. It is better to make judgements after you have heard all the information.

4. You can't listen to anybody's view which disagrees with your own, or take criticism. You will twist facts to suit your own argument.

5. You want to be nice and people to like you but you don't really want to get involved, so you placate them

by saying things like: *'Oh, that's terrible'*, *'I know'*, or *'Oh, yes'*.

6. You respond to whatever is being said with a joke or quip. You are not interested in listening seriously because what they are saying makes you feel uncomfortable in some way.

Ten Ways to Improve Listening Skills

1. Maintain good eye contact.
2. Lean towards speaker slightly.
3. Try to stay relaxed.
4. Keep an open mind – even if you disagree with what's being said.
5. Don't interrupt unless it is to clarify a point by asking questions.
6. Say things like *'yes'*, *'mmm'*, *'I understand'* and nod occasionally.
7. Move away from distractions.
8. Be patient. Allow plenty of time.
9. Show the talker that you want to listen. Look and act interested.
10. Empathise with the talker. Try to put yourself in their shoes, see things from their point of view.

Most people don't realise that it's the listener, not the speaker, who controls a conversation. As an experiment the next time someone is having a conversation with you do this: After a few seconds break eye contact, look at your watch or doodle, lean back in your chair and keep this up for 30 seconds. Then ask the other person how they feel and whether what you were doing affected what they were saying. You will find the speaker says things like, *'I felt I was boring you', 'What I was saying was stupid', 'I tried to change what I was saying to keep you interested'*, etc.

Jim is a manager of a number of people and thinks he is a good listener. When staff come into his office to speak to him he tells them he is listening but at the same time is often writing, shuffling papers and looking down at his desk. He now realises that this could well affect what people are saying to him and give his staff the impression that he is not really listening. From now on he will give good eye contact, stop fiddling with papers and look as though he is actively listening.

Picking up on the Feelings Behind the Words

When listening to another person speaking, try to listen beyond the words. What are the feelings behind the words? If you can pick up on those feelings you could well make the other person feel as if they have really been listened to. For example, at work it can be very difficult to listen to a customer who is complaining in an aggressive way. Our natural reaction is to become defensive and try to calm them down. If you pick up on the feelings behind the words this can often get them in a more cooperative frame of mind. Before asking them to sit down, which often inflames the situation, try saying 'Something has obviously made you very angry, how can I help'. Then listen actively and take appropriate action.

> **Exercise:**
>
> Try spending a whole day actively listening to other people. Recognise the barriers you may be putting up when listening to certain people and try not to put your view until you feel you have really understood theirs.

Summary

- Good listeners get listened to

- Recognise the barriers you put up when listening to certain people and try to avoid them

- Pick up on the feelings behind the words

- Practise active listening

Asking the Right Questions

No two people experience the world in exactly the same way. Everyone sees and explains the world from their own model of the way things are. A famous politician was accused of being out of touch with ordinary people. He denied this by saying he regularly spoke to the employees on his estate. The same words can mean different things to different people. If I say I like relaxing listening to music and to me that means listening to heavy metal, I will have very little in common with you if you relax by listening to opera.

I am sure you have been in a situation where the words didn't come out of your mouth the way you intended. They got lost in the translation somewhere between brain and mouth. Being imprecise or vague with our words can cause miscommunication.

To be effective communicators requires us to use words precisely to ensure the other person understands our meaning. We also need to know as nearly as possible what the other person is meaning and to help them to be clear about what they mean.

Appropriate use of questions can help us gain an accurate understanding of both the facts and the feelings behind a person's meaning.

Open Questions

These questions require fuller answers than just 'yes' or 'no'. They can be phrased in such a way as to initiate a discussion, and thus gain more information from which further questions can be generated.

e.g.   *'What should your manager do to encourage staff to come to her if they have a problem?'*

'What was the boat journey like'?

If you keep quiet and actively listen to the other person's response after asking a question, you will often find people give you more information. If you make encouraging noises like 'yes', 'and', 'carry on' and then keep quiet, people will say even more.

Other ways of starting open questions are: Who? When? Where? Which? Why? How? Tell me about . . .?

You can use open questions to obtain clarification and encourage people to be more specific when they make general or vague statements:

e.g. *'It's unfair'* (Q) *What is unfair?*
      'They don't understand (Q) *Who doesn't understand*
      me'   *you?*
      'I'd like to do that but
      I can't'   (Q) *What stops you?*
      'Fred makes me mad' (Q) *How does he make you*
                                  mad?

Closed Questions

These questions invite the answer 'yes' or 'no' and they are not an effective way of gaining general information. Closed questions are good for checking facts. They are also useful for bringing the conversation back to the point.

Closed questions start like this:

Have you? Is it? Can you? Will you? Could you? Do you?

e.g. *'Have you finished that report yet?'*
      'Is it time to go?'
      'So what you're saying is that you left XYZ Company because there were no promotion prospects. Is that correct?'

Try to avoid asking an open question immediately followed by a closed question. It confuses people and they tend to only answer the closed question:

e.g. *'Why haven't you completed that? Is it because you have too much work?'*

Next time a radio DJ asks you to phone in with an answer to a question which starts *'Do you know . . . ?'*, telephone in with the answer *'Yes'* to claim your prize. He did ask a closed question after all!

Summary

■ Everyone sees and explains the world from their own model of the way things are.

■ Appropriate use of questions can help us gain an accurate understanding of a situation.

■ Use open questions to get clarification and encourage people to give more information.

■ Use closed questions to check facts.

3

Building Rapport

'If you want to win a man to your cause, first convince him that you are his sincere friend.'   **Abraham Lincoln**

Have you ever been in a situation where you meet someone for the first time and after a few minutes' conversation feel as if they are more like friends than strangers. Chances are that you have the same views on a particular issue, similar backgrounds, or something else in common. We use the expression *'I like her, she speaks my kind of language'*, which means *'I like her, she's like me, I can trust her'*.

Rapport is the ability to get on the right wavelength with someone. The Oxford dictionary definition is: *'Communication, relationship, connection.'* It is the ability to be able to enter someone else's world and make them feel you understand them. It is about creating an atmosphere of trust and responsiveness.

When communicating with people you have two choices. You can either emphasise the *differences* between you or choose to emphasise the *similarities* – the things you share. It is very difficult to establish rapport with people if you only emphasise the differences.

How do we create rapport with people? If you observe people who are in rapport, for example good friends at parties or in the pub, you will see that they tend to mirror each other's movements, a bit like a dance. Their body positions will be similar and they will pick up their glasses and drink at the same time.

People with good interpersonal skills create rapport and rapport creates trust. You can create rapport with people by consciously using the natural rapport skills you already have. I am sure you have tried to explain something to a child at some time and found the best way to do this is to squat down to the same level as the child and use words the child can understand. Or when talking to an elderly person you speak slowly, and may change your tone a little and use words they are familiar with.

Listen to the kinds of words and phrases the other person uses, and try to incorporate them into your conversation. I don't mean mimic or copy the other person's accent, but be sensitive to their level of vocabulary. Avoid using in your own speech any jargon that the other person doesn't understand. No-one likes to feel stupid or inferior and someone may reject your ideas because they did not understand the way they were presented.

Attempt to match the other person's body language sensitively and with respect. Do not indiscriminately copy the other person's every movement. If you are sitting or standing put your body position in a similar position to the other person's. You can match arm movements by small hand movements, body movements by your head movements.

Exercise:

Next time you are talking to someone purposely *mismatch* their body position, tone of voice and language. Notice how this feels to you and what impact it has on the conversation. Then match their body position and, if possible, tone and language. Notice how this feels and what impact it has on the conversation.

Summary

- Rapport is the ability to get on the same wavelength as others.

- Emphasise similarities rather than differences.

- Match other people's language and body position sensitively and with respect.

Selecting the Right Response at the Right Time

Knowing how to respond effectively to a variety of situations takes skill and practice. Knowing the outcome you want can help you select the right response. Do you want to develop a mutually cooperative relationship with a work colleague, or handle a customer's complaint without it escalating, or take faulty goods back to a shop and get your money back?

You are more likely to succeed with people if you think about your behaviour and select and use behaviours that help rather than hinder your dealings with other people. There are only two basic rules for successfully selecting the right response. First, you have to give what you would like to receive. This means that the respect, interest and attention you *want* from others must be something you also *give* to others. Second, use visual behaviours which reinforce the things you are saying.

Whether you are talking to people at work, friends, relatives, or customers, research has shown that certain behaviours are more likely to get a favourable reaction.

Ten Ways to Maximise a Favourable Response

1. Move towards the other person at a distance where you can talk and interact comfortably.

2. Lean forward. When you lean away from people they feel you are not interested in them.

3. Uncross your arms and legs, having an open posture makes you look less defensive.

4. Make eye contact If you find looking people in the eye difficult, then look at their eyebrows or nose, the other person won't be able to tell the difference.

5. Smile, everyone understands a smile means you are friendly and open.

6. When the other person speaks show that you are listening by nodding and making appropriate noises.

7. Acknowledge the other person's feelings and point of view

8. Use the other person's name early on in the conversation.

9. Be non-judgemental towards the other person.

10. Admit it when you don't know the answer or have made a mistake

Summary

■ Knowing the outcome you want can help you select the right response.

■ Give what you would like to receive.

■ Use visual behaviours which reinforce your message.

Conclusion

Effective interpersonal skills are essential to personal and professional success. This book is a practical contribution to help you achieve your goals. There is probably very little in this book you don't already know at some level of your experience. Much of what is written is good, common-sense but unfortunately not always common practice. It is now up to you to practise what you have learnt. No-one can make you skilful but yourself, and therefore changing old habits and ways can be difficult. But it is worth reminding yourself that the outcome is worth it – both professionally and socially.

Bibliography

Interpersonal Skills at Work, Maureen Guirdham, Prentice Hall, 1990.

A Woman in Your Own Right, Anne Dickson, Quartet, 1982.

Assertiveness at Work, David R. Stubbs, Pan Books Ltd, 1986.

Improve Your People Skills, Peter Honey, Institute of Personnel Management, 1988.

Getting to Yes, Roger Fisher & William Ury, Hutchinson, 1982.

Peoplemaking, Virginia Satir, Souvenir Press.

Introducing Neuro-Linguistic Programming, Joseph O'Connor & John Seymour, Mandala 1990.

I'm OK, You're OK, Thomas Harris, Pan Books Ltd, 1973.

The Magic of Rapport, Jerry Richardson, Meta Publications, 1987.

Body Language, Allan Pease, Sheldon Press, 1986.